THE MAGIC *of*
SINGAPORE

Contents

Left: *Lush vegetation is evident in a remarkable number of urban parks throughout the island.*

The Land

Resting like a full-stop at the southernmost tip of Peninsular Malaysia, the tropical island of Singapore commands a strategic position in Southeast Asia. To the north, it is linked to Malaysia by a 1km (half-mile) causeway over the Johor Straits, while to the south, across the Straits of Singapore, lies Indonesia, the largest archipelago in the world.

Protected by the rugged mountain ranges of these two giant neighbours, Singapore is spared the brunt of the elements, especially during the monsoon season when rough seas and high winds prevail. Situated approximately 137km (85 miles) north of the equator, Singapore's climate is typically tropical with high average temperatures and humidity tempered by a prevailing cool sea breeze. The heaviest rains fall from November to January during the northeast monsoon season, while intermittent showers provide welcome relief throughout the year. Singapore's combined total landmass is a mere 646km^2 (250 square miles).

Above: *A nostalgic boat ride down the Singapore River* ① *(see map on inside front cover) in a traditional bumboat.*
Right: *Sandy beaches and tranquil waters are part of the appeal of the idyllic islands that surround Singapore.*

The territory consists of the mainland, 42km (26 miles) in length and 23km (14 miles) in breadth, and some 60 tiny islands strewn about its territorial waters, of which more than 20 are inhabited.

Geographically, the island can be divided into three regions: the central hilly region of Bukit Timah, Bukit Gombak and Bukit Mandai; the western region of hills and valleys extending towards the northwest; and the relatively flat eastern region which extends from Katong to Changi. The largest river on the island is the 15km-long (9-mile) Sungei Seletar. In the built-up areas, the natural drainage system of rivers has been replaced by man-made concrete channels. Singapore's highest point, Bukit Timah Hill, is only 163m (535ft) high. Much of the island lies within 15m (49ft) above sea level and the coast is generally flat with the exception of a few cliffs. Reclamation works and swamp clearance have altered the coastline, but the many islands surrounding the mainland offer idyllic sandy beaches.

CLIMATE	
Average temperature:	Day – 31°C (88°F) ; night – 23°C (73°F)
Average humidity:	85%
Annual rainfall:	2360mm (93in)
Northeast monsoon season:	December to February – cooler, windier (40kph; 25 mph) months with higher rainfall
Southwest monsoon season:	June to September – drier, less windy (20kph; 12 mph) conditions
Inter-monsoon periods:	April to May; October to November – a few early morning thunderstorms occur (highest recorded windspeed 144kph; 90 mph)
Sunniest month:	February
Wettest month:	December

Above: *Singapore's landscaped parks are living proof of its superb natural heritage.*
Left: *Characteristic of the island is its combination of sophisticated development and its profusion of tropical greenery and exotic flowering trees.*

Left: *In Bukit Timah Nature Reserve, ② a rather bold long-tailed macaque relishes a half-eaten durian.*

Flora and Fauna

Once covered in lowland rainforest and rich mangrove swamps, Singapore has been irrevocably altered by human interference; the ancient tracts of primary rainforest that were the island's natural heritage have made way for massive urban development. Thirty years after the founding of Singapore in 1819, more than half of the virgin rainforest was still intact but, by 1854, these forests had become severely depleted due largely to Singapore's status as a flourishing trade station. Laws for the protection of nature, such as the Forest Reserve Act of 1882, failed to curb the tide of deforestation to supply the booming timber trade. By 1935, many of the forest reserves established in 1884 had been wiped out. Wide-scale deforestation continued long after the era of British colonialism came to a close in 1959, 14 years after World War II, largely due to the demands of nation building which began in earnest in the 1960s. Since separating from Malaysia and becoming a fully sovereign nation in 1965, Singapore has been transformed into a newly industrialized economy; this, together with an expanding population, has not resulted, however, in the wholesale destruction of nature. Today, pockets of natural or semi-natural vegetation still exist in the 4.5% of land area dedicated to nature conservation. One such protected area is the Bukit Timah Nature Reserve. Granted official protection as a nature

Above: *The Singapore Zoological Gardens ③ arguably have the largest colony of captive orang-utans anywhere in the world. These apes are endemic to the rain-forests of Borneo and parts of Sumatra.*

reserve under the Nature Reserves Ordinance in 1951, Bukit Timah comprises 81 ha (200 acres) of primary lowland rainforest. Beneath the forest canopy of giant trees, mainly of the Dipterocarp family (species with two-winged seeds), are well-marked walking trails that lure visitors into a lush landscape of more than 850 species of flowering plants and inhabited by brightly coloured birds and butterflies, monkeys, lemurs and squirrels. The present government's resolve to make the island a model garden city has the full support of Singaporeans who are acutely aware of the importance of living in a clean and green environment. Around 80% of the flora that beautifies and creates shade in public parks and gardens and along roads is

introduced; most decorative plants are exotic flowering species such as the frangipani from Mexico and the raintree (*Samanea saman*), bougainvillaea and lantana from South America.

Over the centuries, human encroachment has effectively wiped out many of Singapore's larger mammals (tigers, elephants, wild boar, civet cats and leopards). In the first quarter of the 19th century, tigers were so widespread that they presented a serious problem to the invading human hordes who were taking over their habitat. But their reign was short-lived: the last tiger was shot at Choa Chu Kang Village in 1930. Among the more common mammals still to be seen in the reserve areas and parks are the plantain squirrel, long-tailed macaque, flying lemur, lesser mousedeer and pangolin. At Singapore's Zoological Gardens, an impressive zoo set in 90ha (220 acres) of pristine parkland, visitors can see everything from orang-utans to the Indonesian Komodo dragons.

Many unique lowland rainforest bird species like trogons, nuthatches, broadbills, hornbills, pittas and pheasants have been replaced by more common and adaptable urban and garden bird species such as mynahs, sparrows, crows and some bulbuls. Today, about 326 species of birds are found in Singapore of which only 215 are local species. During the migratory season, waders and birds of prey arrive from the northern climes and find protection in the Sungei Buloh Nature Park, a sanctuary with mangrove boardwalks and bird observation hides.

Singapore's nature reserves, including Bukit Timah and the Central Water Catchment Area which incorporates the park surrounding MacRitchie Reservoir, are managed by the National Parks Board (NParks), which was established on 6 June 1990.

Above: *There are many stunning orchid species growing in the National Orchid Enclosure in the Botanic Gardens.* ④

Left: *This striking ginger flower (*Hornstedtia scyphifera*) grows deep in the forest of Bukit Timah Nature Reserve.* **Above:** *The attractive green agamid lizard, or 'false chameleon', is frequently encountered at the edge of the forest.* **Below:** *A female olive-backed sunbird (*Nectarinia jugularis*) feeds its young.*

Left: *Wax models in the Wax Museum depict Japan's formal surrender to the British on 12 September 1945 at the Council Chamber of the Municipal Building (now the City Hall).*

History

Written accounts of Singapore's ancient history are somewhat sketchy, but the basis of all references begins with its modern-day founding by Sir Stamford Raffles who sailed into the mouth of the Singapore River on 29 January 1819 to establish a trading station under an agreement between the British East India Company and the Sultan of Johor, the Malay ruler of the island.

Raffles quickly realized the strategic importance of the ruins of a 45m-high (148ft) hill ('Forbidden Hill' or Bukit Larangan as it had been known earlier) and established his residence there. This hill had once been the throne of the rulers of the ancient city of Temasek and was used in the 14th century to repel ferocious attacks by invaders from Siam (now Thailand) to the north. Temasek later came to be known as Singapura ('Lion City'), although the origin of this name is not exactly clear. Until the arrival of European steamships with their superior guns and greater speed, the swamp-infested island was known largely as a pirate base and on 19th-century maps of the region it was noted and marked that it be approached with caution.

Recognizing the island's potential to become a vital and strategically located centre in Southeast Asia, Raffles set about transforming Singapore into a flourishing trading port. The settlement's development was carefully planned along scientific lines with proper regulation of land. Eventually a town-planning committee was set up and a commercial centre built to facilitate the flow of businesses. Within four months of its founding, the town's population grew from 120 Malays and 30 Chinese to 5000. By 1824, when the first census was taken, the population had swelled to 10,683.

Upon Raffles' resignation and subsequent return to England in 1823, Singapore was placed in the hands of the Supreme Government of India. In 1824, Singapore was ceded in perpetuity to the British East India Company by the Sultan of Johor and became a British possession. Two years later, together with Penang and Melaka, it became one of the 'Straits Settlements' with administrative headquarters based in Penang. In 1867, the Straits Settlements were ceded to the British Colonial Office and became a crown colony. The British surrender to Japanese forces in 1942 marked a new era in the history of modern Singapore for it wit-

Above: *A statue of the modern-day founder of Singapore, Sir Stamford Raffles, who sailed up the Singapore River ① on 29 January 1819.*

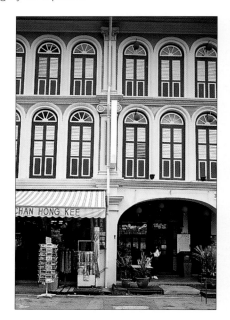

Above: *In Chinatown, ⑤ rows of pre-war shophouses have been restored as part of a conservation programme by the Urban Redevelopment Authority (URA); it aims to preserve the Chinese legacy for future generations.*

Above: *These
prewar shophouses
along South Bridge
Road were built by
Chinese migrants
in their distinct
architectural style.
Many old buildings
have been restored
and transformed into
upmarket offices.*

nessed the triumph of an Asian power over a seemingly invincible European one. But Japan's conquest did not last long. In September 1945, shortly after the Soviet Union's declaration of war against Japan and the dropping of the atomic bombs on Hiroshima and Nagasaki, the Japanese Imperial Army surrendered to the British. Singapore was reoccupied by the Allied powers under Supreme Commander Lord Mountbatten and British colonial rule returned. Soon after, in 1946, Singapore became a separate crown colony.

The first Legislative Council election took place on 20 March 1948, resulting in six local leaders being included in the council. In 1953, a commission, under Sir George Rendel, which was appointed to review Singapore's constitutional position and make recommendations for change, had its proposals accepted by the government and in 1955, the Rendel Constitution resulted in a form of self-government for Singapore. At the first general elections, in 1959, the People's Action Party (PAP), led by Mr Lee Kuan Yew, won 43 of the 51 seats in the Legislative Assembly which later became the Parliament. Mr Lee became the first prime minister and the nation achieved internal self-government. On 3 June, the governor, Sir William Gode, was elected the first Yang di-Pertuan Negara, or Head of State, under the new constitution and on 5 June, the first government was officially sworn in.

Malaya, Sabah, Sarawak and Singapore united to form Malaysia on 16 September 1963, but the merger was to be short-lived. Singapore separated from Malaysia in 1965 and became a fully sovereign state and a republic on 22 December of that year. Under Mr Lee Kuan Yew's dynamic leadership, the island became one of the most talked-about economic success stories of modern times. Mr Lee, the longest serving prime minister in the world, stepped down in 1990 and was succeeded by Mr Goh Chok Tong.

Below: *This wax
tableau depicts the
many Indian and
Chinese migrants who
came to Singapore as
labourers, toiling day
and night to make
ends meet.*

Government and Economy

Singapore is a republic with a parliamentary system of government. The organs of the state – the executive, the legislature and the judiciary – are provided for by a written constitution and the president is the head of state. The administration of the government is handled by the cabinet which is led by the prime minister, all of whom are appointed by the president from among the members of parliament. In January 1991, the constitution was amended to make it possible for Singapore citizens to elect a president, who holds office for a fixed term of six years. The first presidential election took place on 28 August 1993. In 1999, President S R Nathan took office after an uncontested election.

Singapore is one of the few countries in the world to enjoy such a high standard of living. It is also one of the few nations that does not have any foreign debt. The general literacy rate is about 91%, virtually every household owns a television and Singapore has the greatest number of computers in the world in relation to its population size.

Left: *The development of the MRT (Mass Rapid Transport), by reducing the number of annoying traffic jams in the city, has enhanced the productivity of Singapore's businesspeople.*

Below: *Boat Quay is a favourite haunt of tourists. This stretch of the Singapore River ① has been a great success since the intensive clean-up of the once polluted waterway.*

SINGAPORE SUCCESSES

- Singapore's Changi Airport was voted the world's best airport in 1994 by several international business travel magazines.
- Singapore Airlines (SIA) has won the 'best-of-the-best' award for over two decades.
- The Port of Singapore Authority (PSA) was rated the second busiest port in the world in terms of shipping tonnage in 1995 according to a report by *Cargo News Asia*.
- Singapore was rated as the most competitive economy on earth by the World Competitiveness Report.
- The Singapore workforce was rated as the best in the world in 1994 by the Washington-based Business Environment Risk Intelligence (BERI).
- *Fortune* magazine voted Singapore as the 'world's number one city for business' in November 1995.

Above: *The Stock Exchange of Singapore (SES) is governed by a body of no more than 13 directors who are either stockbroking or non-stockbroking members.*

Over 85% of the population lives in Housing Development Board (HDB) flats and 82% owns them. Although biotechnology is Singapore's latest thriving sector, its healthy economy has also been attributed to an upswing in the electronics industry as well as buoyant regional growth. The manufacturing, commerce, transport and communications sections have generally performed well, while the launch of Windows '95 particularly boosted the electronics sector and increased production of personal computers, disk drives, CD-ROM drives and printers.

The Singapore Tourist Board (STB) was established in 1964 with the aim of developing and promoting tourism on the island. Besides being an internationally important centre for trade and communications, Singapore is considered the gateway to Southeast Asia. Offering sophisticated tourist facilities, an excellent transportation system, fabulous shopping, tempting cuisine, a vibrant nightlife, an enthralling melée of cultures, and fascinating history, Singapore is an enticing holiday destination.

Above: *In terms of shipping tonnage, Singapore is the second busiest port in the world.* **Below:** *The World Trade Centre, ⑥ opposite Sentosa Island, ⑦ was upgraded at a cost of S$116 million, and ranks as a top international exhibition and convention centre.*

Left: *English is the most widely spoken of all languages on the island, and is also the main medium of instruction in schools. All students must learn a second language, be it Mandarin, Malay or Tamil.*

The People

Singapore is essentially a migrant society and one of the most cosmopolitan countries in Asia. It is a secular state with a multiracial and multicultural mix; every ethnic community is entitled to practise its own respective religion and way of life. This unifying policy has resulted in a rich cultural heritage with a fascinating array of customs and festivals that are celebrated throughout the year. This blend of cultural traditions, while retaining the essential roots of each culture and religion, has taken on a distinctive Singaporean flavour.

The people of Singapore are largely descendants of immigrants from the Malay Peninsula, China, the Indian subcontinent, Sri Lanka and Arabia. A small percentage are Eurasians – a racial mix of Europeans, Malays, Arabs, Chinese and Indians. As Singapore gradually turned into a thriving free port, people from the older settlement of Melaka also came flocking to the island.

The first Chinese junk arrived in February 1821 and by the mid-1800s immigration had become highly organized. Most immigrants were men who came in search of a better life. They had to live under the protection of the various dialect clan associations and secret society brotherhoods. As a result of the costs incurred on their long voyage, many of them started their new life in debt. Often they were exploited and badly treated, although the indentured labour system was fortunately abolished in 1914. By the 1870s, the favourable government policies began to encourage more Chinese women.

Many Straits- and China-born immigrants settled permanently in Singapore with the four major dialect groups being the Cantonese, Teochews, Hokkiens and Hakkas. A few prominent Chinese merchants became British subjects as a result of the naturalization law, which was passed in 1852. The Chinese population expanded very quickly and by 1830, the Chinese outnumbered the Malays, a trend that remains to this day. By 1867, they totalled 67% of the population, numbering 55,000; this grew to 250,000 by 1912. While considerable numbers settled permanently in Singapore, many of them left the country after a brief period of stay.

Modern-day Indian immigration began with the founding of

Below: *Buddhism was originally brought to Singapore by Chinese immigrants, and today there are many fine Buddhist temples which propagate the teachings and rituals of this religion.*

Above: *Skilled calligraphers practise their art on red rice paper; the gold Chinese characters usually emphasize good fortune, good health, posterity and prosperity.*

Singapore: on the day Raffles stepped ashore in 1819, he was accompanied by 120 Indian soldiers and an Indian trader. Later, employment opportunities and liberal policies towards immigration attracted many Indian immigrants who were teachers, clerks, technicians and traders. Several hundred Indian convicts were also brought in as construction workers to build roads and bridges (among the buildings constructed by convicts were Sri Mariamman Temple, the Istana and St Andrew's Cathedral). Indentured labourers, too, were brought in from south India to build railways, canals, wharves and other essential public works. Although the indentured labour system was abolished in 1914, Indian immigration continued. South Indians are still by far the largest ethno-linguistic group from India, forming 80% of Indian immigrants in Singapore.

In the 184 years since its founding, the population of this bustling city has grown tremendously from a mere 150 people living along the banks of the Singapore River to around 4.02 million in 2002.

For a taste of modern Singaporean life, visitors should pop in at Lau Pa Sat, housed in an ornate Victorian filigree cast-iron building. Once a wet market, it has been restored and transformed into a hawker market with free cultural performances taking place virtually every night, and food stalls serving local cuisine alfresco style. Clarke Quay, situated alongside the Singapore River, is another lively venue where the streets are filled with musicians and pushcart vendors peddling souvenirs.

Right: *There are two important annual events on the Muslim calendar: Hari Raya Puasa, which takes place at the end of Ramadan, the month of fasting and alms-giving, and Hari Raya Haji, which is celebrated a day after the Haj Pilgrims converge in the holy city of Mecca to perform major rites of the pilgrimage.*

Religions and Festivals

Islam was the first religion to come to Singapore. For many centuries, traders from Islamic countries like Arabia and Persia brought with them their great faith which soon spread throughout the Malay Peninsula and all of Indonesia.

Buddhism and Taoism The early Chinese settlers brought these religious practices to Singapore and they have been passed down through generations (the majority of Buddhists are of Chinese origin). Their form of Buddhism is traditionally blended with Taoism and Confucianism. Most Buddhists belong to the Mahayana school, followed by Thervada and others. In recent years, Buddhist organizations have adopted a more modern outlook in their structures and methods in order to meet the demands of an increasingly sophisticated populace.

Christianity Introduced to Singapore at the beginning of the 19th century largely by Portuguese and French missionaries, both Catholic and Protestant communities exist, but the Protestants arrived much earlier and had the largest following.

Hinduism Like the Chinese, early Indian Hindu immigrants, mostly from south India, established their traditions by building many temples across the island. Hindus are deeply influenced by their religion, which involves many complex rituals and

Above: *A few of the Buddhist temples in Singapore, such as the Thian Hock Seng and Siong Lim temples, are national monuments that continue to serve the religious and cultural needs of the Buddhist community.*

Left: *St Andrew's Cathedral, situated in the heart of the city in Coleman Street, was designed by Colonel Ronald MacPherson; Indian convicts built the cathedral between 1856 and 1864.*

the temple is the most important venue for their festivals and ceremonies. Every devout Hindu family has a prayer room and an altar in their home.

Other religions The Sikhs from northern India are an important ethnic group in Singapore. Although their numbers are small, there are 16 registered Sikh religious and social organizations, some of which run their own Gurdawara, or Sikh temples. The Jewish faith is represented by two synagogues in Singapore.

Festivals Singapore's vibrant and colourful multiracial society results in many festivals. Among those celebrated by the Chinese are Lunar New Year in January or February and Qing Ming, which takes place in April and is a time for remembrance of ancestors. The Yu Lan Jie, or Feast of the Hungry Ghost, is observed in mid-August in which the dead are again remembered. The mid-autumn festival falls on the 15th day of the eighth lunar month in the Chinese calendar.

The Muslims have two major festivals. Hari Raya Puasa, or Aidil Fitri, takes place at the end of Ramadan, marking a month of fasting, alms-giving and abstinence. Hari Raya Haji is a time for remembrance, sacrifice and prayer and is celebrated a day after Haj pilgrims converge in the holy city of Mecca.

The Buddhists observe Vesak Day, which falls on the day of the full moon in May. It commemorates the birth, enlightenment and Nirvana of the Buddha. Celebrations are marked by mass candlelight processions.

Celebration of the Tamil New Year is variable – some Indian groups observe it early in the year, while others do so at other times. During Thaipusam, a

Below: Dragons are common in the Chinese community, where they are regarded as friendly symbols of good luck.

Below right: The magnificent Masjid Sultan Mosque in Bussorah Street was built by British architects to grand Arabic design and scale, complete with domes, minarets and balustrades.

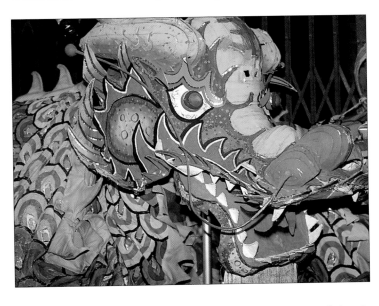

Right: The 1827 Sri Mariamman Temple, located in South Bridge, is the oldest and most opulent Hindu temple in Singapore.

penitential festival in honour of Lord Subramaniam that takes place between January and February, devotees carry *kavadi* (wooden frames) and pierce sharp skewers through their tongues, cheeks and bodies. The delightful Deepavali, the festival of lights, is celebrated by Hindus and Sikhs.

For Christians, the most notable ceremony is Christmas. During this time, the entire length of Orchard Road is lined with a kaleidoscope of lights, vibrant colours and festive displays. Other festivals in the Christian calendar, such as Good Friday and Easter Sunday, are also celebrated in Singapore.

DOWNTOWN SINGAPORE

Bright city lights, ultra-modern shopping complexes, fine restaurants and internationally renowned hotels, indoor air-conditioned hawker centres, and cinemas – these are just some of the wonders of city life condensed into world-famous Orchard Road. Explore the city by foot to ensure that you do not miss a single shopping outlet. In terms of delectable food, virtually every nationality in the world is represented on the streets of Singapore. The nightlife is enticing too, with enough pubs, bars, cafés, discos, and lounges to cater to everybody's taste. Singapore does not have topless bars or X-rated girlie shows, but no one needs them anyway. With a year-round carnival atmosphere, there are lots of other things on offer in this city of friendly people where the streets are filled with locals and visitors from every part of the world.

Above: *A bird's-eye view of the famous Orchard Road with its hotels, and shopping and entertainment centres.* **Right:** *The 73-storey Swissôtel The Stamford is the tallest hotel in Singapore.* **Opposite:** *On Sunday mornings, you would be forgiven for mistaking the Lucky Plaza for a 'Little Philippines', as thousands of Filipino women congregate here for their day off from their domestic duties as maids in Singaporean households.*

14

Left: *Wisma Atria, with its modern design and excellent facilities, caters for the comfort of tourists and local shoppers.*

Below: *Orchard Road is the top shopping destination for most tourists; cameras and electronic goods are well priced here.* **Bottom:** *The Forum Galleria, which conveniently adjoins the Orchard MRT Station at basement level, also enjoys a high reputation among tourists.* **Opposite:** *Isetan Scotts at Orchard Road Shaw House epitomizes the architectural design of many of Singapore's shopping complexes with a blend of aesthetics, comfort and grandeur – and total convenience.*

Left: Hotels and shopping complexes of increasingly innovative design abound in Singapore. The Glass Hotel's 'hanging lifts' provoke terror in those with a fear of heights, and excitement for thrill-seekers.

Opposite: Experience the shopping frenzy of a lifetime, or spend delightful evenings sipping wine and enjoying dinner at one of the innumerable open cafés situated along Orchard Road.
Left: Located right in the heart of Orchard Road, Centrepoint Shopping Centre is one of the most popular shopping destinations on the island.
Below: Takashimaya, an upmarket department store, is housed in Ngee Ann City currently home to more than 140 tenants.

Above: *This row of old houses in Emerald Hill Road is a historical conservation site with a distinctive Peranakan flavour. Peranakans are Straits-born Chinese who have adopted some Malay ways, particularly their language (with some dissimilarities) and style of dress.* **Above right:** *An example of an intricately carved door typically seen in houses in Emerald Hill Road.*

Left: *The Orchard Emerald, situated next to the well-known Peranakan Place and close to the Centrepoint shopping complex, offers the visitor a chance to unwind with a cold beer and delicious local food to the sounds of a live band.*
Opposite: *An example of the antique shops that specialize in fine antiques from Southeast Asia and India. The Indian collection depicted here is interesting because it features architectural pieces from several Indian palaces.*

THE COLONIAL HEART

It was from the Singapore River – lifeline, link and legacy – that the island city-state of Singapore grew and expanded inland. The very pillars of the nation's economic success are evident in the impressive concentration of major buildings that line the waterfront and Shenton Way in the financial district. A stroll along the historic river is equivalent to a walk through Singapore's past, present and future. The statue of Stamford Raffles is situated near Parliament House on the precise spot where the island's modern founder landed on 29 January 1819. Indeed, an excellent way of following the history of Singapore is to take a river cruise from Parliament Steps or Liang Court in a Chinese bumboat.

Top: *The Padang, with the Supreme Court in the background, is a very popular ground for sports matches.* **Right:** *Cricket remains a popular sport in Singapore.*

Left: *The Victoria Memorial Hall, built in 1905, was renovated during the 1970s and is now a major concert hall.*
Opposite: *The Supreme Court, built between 1937 and 1939, features a Corinthian terrazzo, an Ionic column and a Tympanum sculpture, which are all the work of master Italian craftsman, Cavalori Rudolfo Nolli.*

Previous pages: *Singapore by night, with the Victoria Theatre and Memorial Hall, the Singapore Cricket Club, the Padang, the dome of the Supreme Court, and Boat Quay clearly visible.* **Above left:** *An exhibition of the Malay Wayang Kulit, or shadow puppet play, at the Singapore History Museum.* **Above right:** *An example of a puppet show from China at a Chinese cultural exhibition.* **Opposite:** *A replica of the Qing Dynasty (1644–1911) Chinese dragon robe, traditionally worn by the Chinese emperor.* **Below:** *Interpret it whichever way you want: this artwork showing life-sized figures outside the Singapore History Museum is the labour of love of Taiwanese artist, Ju Ming.*

Left: *A permanent exhibit near the entrance to the National Museum is this 19th-century Garuda wood sculpture from Tamil Nadu in southern India; it is a vehicle for the Hindu god Vishnu.*

Above and below: *The Raffles Hotel, with its rarified colonial ambience, is, perhaps, the most sought-after rendezvous of the rich and famous. Over the years, great personalities, including Somerset Maugham and Noel Coward, have been guests here.* **Bottom:** *The multimillion-dollar facelift which the hotel underwent in recent years has not detracted from its refined atmosphere.*

Opposite: *This ornate, 6m-high (20ft) cast-iron fountain is one of only two in Singapore, and was originally built in the 1890s. It is located in the delightful Palm Garden, which is in the main building of the Raffles Hotel.*

Above left: *This teapot is an example of the wide range of Chinese porcelain featured in specialist shops in the huge Raffles City Shopping Centre.* **Above right:** *At this modern centre, you can literally 'shop till you drop' – such is the variety of goods on display.* **Opposite:** *An interior view of the Raffles City Shopping Centre, regarded as one of Singapore's premier retail areas.* **Bottom:** *Free, colourful performances are sometimes staged on the concourse in Raffles City.*

Right, top: *A leisurely meal next to the blissfully cool Singapore River is highly recommended. Choose from a wide selection of Eastern and Western cuisine.*

Right, centre: *Asian, Middle Eastern, European, or even American – whatever your choice of food, you will find it at one of the many restaurants situated at Boat Quay.*

Bottom: *Once the sun has set, Boat Quay comes alive; the nightlife usually does not end until the early hours of the morning.* **Opposite:** *At sundown, the city centre is transformed into a dazzling landscape of glittering lights.*

Following pages: *There is no need to fear the dark in Singapore; with one of the lowest crime rates in Asia, it is safe to walk the streets even at midnight.*

Left: *The Merlion, located adjacent to One Fullerton, symbolizes Singapore's reputation as the 'Lion City'.*

Above: *Boat Quay's elegantly restored prewar shophouses still retain a magical nostalgia, despite the encroachment of the modern world.*

Opposite: *Framed by the fronds of pretty palm trees, the Singapore River ① is abuzz with boating activities.* **Below:** *Wooden bumboats, once used for carrying cargo, are an inexpensive means of transport down the Singapore River.* **Bottom:** *Reflections in the river emphasize the harmonious blend of the old and the new in this vibrant city.*

Above: *Also situated along the Singapore River ① is the lively festival village of Clarke Quay, a feast of dining, entertainment and shopping.*

Above: *Originally from Madagascar, the ubiquitous traveller's palm can be seen along the walkways and boulevards of Singapore; it does not flower in these climatic conditions, but propagates itself by means of suckers which arise from the base of the parent plant.* **Opposite:** *Sometimes, you can have the whole Singapore River to yourself — but only if you are very early.*

Following pages: *At the Clarke Quay, more than 60 shophouses and godowns (warehouses) have been transformed into 170 retail outlets and more than 20 exclusive restaurants and pubs.*

Right: *A statue of Singapore's modern-day founding father, Sir Stamford Raffles, is a landmark on the busy waterfront.*

39

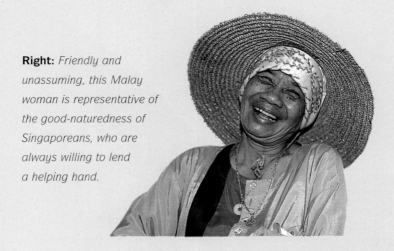

Right: *Friendly and unassuming, this Malay woman is representative of the good-naturedness of Singaporeans, who are always willing to lend a helping hand.*

PEOPLE OF SINGAPORE

Singapore is a cosmopolitan society with a multiracial mix of, among others, Chinese, Malays and Indians, all living in harmony with each other. Thanks to its key geographical position, and subsequent status as a flourishing trading post, migrants and merchants were lured from far and wide to Singapore's shores. Their different cultures, languages and customs formed the basis of the rich cultural mix that is characteristic of Singaporean society today. Singaporeans are among the friendliest people you will ever meet, with smiles that are contagious. It is a rarity to meet someone who does not understand English, and despite the frenetic pace of life in the city, there will always be somebody to help you find your way or answer your questions.

This page: *The people of Singapore — Chinese, Malay, Tamil, Hindu and Buddhist — have acquired a distinctive national identity without relinquishing their religious practices, customs and festivals.*
Opposite: *An Indian man, comfortably dressed in a traditional sarong, reads a copy of Singapore's only Tamil newspaper, the* Tamil Murasu, *outside the Sri Krishnan Temple on Waterloo Street.*

Top: *Traditional Indian souvenirs and curios are popular with shoppers who visit the vibrant Little India Arcade.* ⑧
Above: *Gold shops, like this one in Little India, offer competitively priced jewellery.*

Opposite: *A dazzling array of brightly-coloured sarees on display in a shop in Serangoon Road.*

Left: *For some tourists the sight of Hindu devotees' tongues and bodies pierced by sharp skewers attached to huge metal kavadi in acts of self-mortification, is not entirely pleasant. All this is part of Thaipusam, a penitential festival which is held in honour of Lord Subramaniam in the Tamil month of Thai (between January and February each year).*

Left: *Arab Street is predominantly a Muslim area, with rows of shops selling traditional clothing, baskets, silverware and other goods.*

Left, centre: *Sweet-smelling garlands of jasmine, roses and marigolds, used to decorate altars or as personal adornment, are sold by hawkers in little colourful stores .*

Below: *A profusion of traditional rattan and bamboo products, including chairs, baskets and bins, spills out onto the pavement from this shop-house in Arab Street.*

Opposite: *The choice of imported and locally made material is vast. Bolts of colourful, richly textured or silky smooth cloth are made up into Malay sarongs and modern Western-style dresses.*

Following pages: *The Malabar Mosque, located near Jalan Sultan at the crossroads of North Bridge Road, was built by Indian labourers and serves the Indian Muslim community.*

Above: *The smiling Buddha is a sought-after good luck charm by traditional Chinese Buddhists. Sculptures, such as these fine examples being displayed, are readily available in Chinatown.* **Below:** *Ancient Chinese traditions such as bargaining for goods are still alive in the bustling, noisy streets of Chinatown.* **Bottom:** *At night, shops and Chinatown sidewalks come alive with festive lights and music.*

Opposite: *The name 'Chinatown' suggests a predominantly Chinese population, as do the neat rows of traditional Chinese shophouses in this area. The community, however, is home to other ethnic groups as well.*

Left: *The heady aromas of fruit, spices and flowers pervade the senses and are an integral feature of the many street stalls in the city's downtown areas.*

Opposite: *Eating alfresco on the street is a way of life in Singapore. Both in the city and in the neighbouring housing estates, there are plenty of open-air eating places. In fact, looking for a place to eat is never a problem, but deciding on one can be difficult!*

Left: *There is nothing quite like fresh coconut milk when you need to quench your thirst. In recent years, there has been a significant increase in the number of stores selling freshly squeezed fruit juices, especially along Orchard Road.*

Right: *Lush tropical fruits are abundant in the fresh-produce markets. Besides local favourites like pineapples and bananas, imported apples, mangoes and pears are always available.*

Right: *Durians are a treat if you are used to their pungent smell and flavour. But be warned: it may take a while to acquire a taste for this rich fruit with its creamy texture.*

Left and bottom: *Private housing is very expensive in Singapore. With an average condominium costing over S$1 million, and a semi-detached house fetching well over S$2 million, it is understandable that only 13% of Singaporeans are able to afford their own home. As part of a conservation plan, many important old houses, with unique characteristics and special historical significance, are skilfully renovated to keep their traditional value.*

Left: *Alkaff Mansion, ⑨ or Mount Washington as it was formerly known, was built on Mount Faber Ridge by the wealthy Alkaff family. Today, it is an upmarket restaurant.*

Opposite: *Clean, colourful washing flutters in the sky. This method of hanging clothes out to dry, sometimes referred to as 'flagpole laundry', is a unique characteristic of Singapore's Housing and Development Board (HDB) estates.*

SOUTH OF THE CITY

The serene Botanic Gardens are not far from the top end of Orchard Road. A little further from the city centre are the gently undulating ridges of Mount Faber, with a lookout point offering breathtaking views of Singapore's busy port and nearby Sentosa Island. The World Trade Centre serves as an exciting gateway to the carefree holiday islands of Sentosa, Kusu and St John's, which all lie south of the mainland. Ferries and luxury cruise liners depart from the Singapore Cruise Centre for exotic destinations, including the Indonesian islands of Bintan and Batam. Take a cable car from Mount Faber to Sentosa; on a clear day, the views across the city and out to sea are captivating.

Above: *Covering a distance of 1.85km (1 mile), the aerial network between Mount Faber ⑩ and Sentosa Island ⑦ has transported a great number of passengers since its inception in 1974.*

Opposite: *Over 100 international trade and consumer shows take place every year in the World Trade Centre's ⑥ exhibition halls.*
Left: *From the World Trade Centre you can take a pleasure-boat cruise to Singapore's southern islands.*

Top: *A ferocious 4.5m-long (15ft) dragon greets visitors to the Dragon Court, which is close to the cable car station.*

Above: *The picturesque resort of Sentosa Island is favoured by locals when they need to escape the bustle of the city*

Opposite: *'Sheer magic' is an apt description of the Musical Fountain on Sentosa Island, ⑦ an aesthetic piece of brilliant engineering. It features integrated lights, lasers and colours, together with 20m-high (66ft) water jets set to music.*

Following pages: *From the cable car, ⑪ one has the sensation of being a bird in flight, with a thrilling bird's-eye view of the whole of Sentosa Island.*

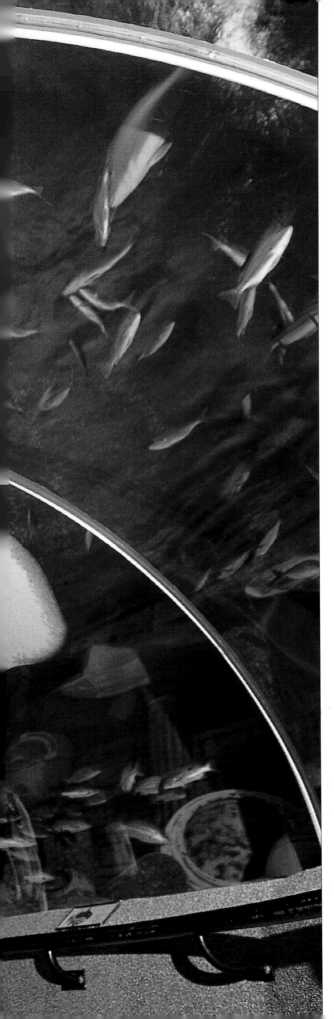

Opposite: *Stingrays, sharks and other interesting creatures of the sea can be seen at Underwater World, Asia's largest tropical fish oceanarium outside the Australasian region.* **Below, top:** *Here at the Images of Festivals, a life-sized model of a Hindu devotee is seen carrying a* kavadi *during the festival of Thaipusam.* **Below, centre:** *A remarkable attention to detail in* Wayang, *a classical Chinese opera characterized by elaborate costumes, head-gear and make-up.* **Below, bottom:** *An awesome three-dimensional hologram of a shark at Underwater World.*

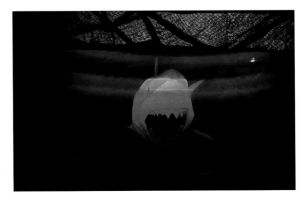

Above: *The tropical charm of these water-lily ponds is typical of the tranquil layout of the Botanic Gardens, ⓘ situated just a short distance from Singapore's bustling city centre, with its familiar roar of traffic.* **Opposite:** *The peaceful gazebo is complemented by the lush greenery and the wonderful scent of cheerful flowers, making this a favourite spot to calm the soul.*

Left: *A well-loved feature of the Botanic Gardens is this statue of a young girl on a bicycle, set among a profusion of flowers.*

Below: *The orchid garden within the Botanic Gardens is a popular attraction that features spectacular displays of exotic orchid species.*

Left: *A highly skilled craftswoman puts the final touches to a pottery vase at Ming Village ⑫ pottery centre.*

WEST OF THE CITY

Jurong, Singapore's most important industrial region, is enhanced by a number of tourist attractions, scattered at a comfortable distance between the housing estates, and well served by MRT trains and connecting buses. Here you will find, among other places, the Jurong Bird Park, which contains the world's largest aviaries; Ming Village, where hard-working craftspeople produce pottery not only for the local market, but increasingly for the foreign market; and Tang Dynasty City, a gigantic cultural theme park. Holland Village, an elegant neighbourhood inhabited by the large expatriate community and by locals, is situated a little closer to the city.

Left: *Holland Village ⑬ is surrounded by a large community of expatriates who live in beautiful free-standing houses. As a result, there is a high concentration of exclusive shopping centres with specialist stores and restaurants in the vicinity.*

Below left: *Ming Village is the largest remaining pottery centre of its kind in Singapore; there are literally thousands of high-quality pieces of art on display.*

Opposite: *Wet markets are typical throughout Singapore. Fresh vegetables, meat and fish are readily available, and at prices that are normally lower than those charged in supermarkets.*

Above: *Performed to the accompaniment of deafening drums, the lion dance is present in every important Chinese celebration. One or two acrobats inside the lion costume show off their skills.*

Opposite: *Venture into the eerie world of Chinese myths and legends at Haw Par Villa, ⑭ a magical 9.5ha (23-acre) wonderland of mind-boggling colourful sculptures depicting the oriental mythological world.*
Below: *A scene from Chinese mythology is vividly depicted in this series of sculptures at the Haw Par Villa.* **Bottom:** *Dragon World is a 'must-see' exhibit. Other attractions include Creation of the World, Legends and Heroes, and Spirit of the Orient Theatre.*

Top: *A row of flags catches the breeze on a bridge leading to the traditional Chinese Garden, ⑮ which provides a peaceful haven for city-dwellers.*

Above: *The Yu Hwa Yuan, situated on a 13.5ha (33-acre) island within Jurong Lake, ⑰ is a delightful place for a leisurely walk. Afterwards, pause a while to enjoy the exhibits of Chinese traditions and beliefs on display.*

Opposite: *Sip Chinese tea, relax and enjoy the serene environment that surrounds the Moon-Inviting Boat, a quiet spot in the Chinese Garden.*

Previous pages: *Climb up the Moon-Receiving Tower or Cloud-Wrapped Pavilion (Twin Towers) to appreciate the beauty of the Chinese Garden at Jurong Lake. It is built to the design and style of the Sung Dynasty in China.*

Left and bottom right: *Colourful South American macaws, the star attraction at the entrance to the Jurong Bird Park, ⑱ perform tricks to entertain the waiting crowds. The macaw is just one of the 8000 birds representing 600 species in the park.*

Left: *The Birds of Prey Show, which is staged twice a day in the Fuji Enclosure, features hawks and eagles; among them is this American bald eagle. The birds demonstrate spectacular hunting dives.*

Left: *Flamingos are amongst the most graceful and attractive of the exhibits at the Jurong Bird Park.*

Opposite: *The grand JBP All-Star Pool Amphitheatre is the main venue for the four immensely popular bird shows held daily at the Jurong Bird Park.*

NORTH AND EAST OF THE CITY

Leave the city's skyscrapers and traffic congestion behind, and head for the Singapore Zoological Gardens in the north. Here, the popular Animal Show, which is staged four times a day, offers visitors the chance to see elephants, sea lions, orang-utans, chimpanzees, and snakes at close quarters. The unique Night Safari is the first of its kind in the world where visitors can view more than 1200 birds and nocturnal animals such as tigers and leopards in their natural habitat. Close by is Malaysia, a popular weekend retreat for Singaporeans who wish to escape the pressure and pace of the city. To the east is Changi Village, a community of relaxed outdoor cafés and pubs, and the gateway to the adventure island, Pulau Ubin. Finally, after a satisfying holiday in Singapore, you head to Changi Airport, voted 'the best airport in the world'.

Opposite: *Enthusiastic crowds congregate to enjoy the highly educational Animal Show in the modern amphitheatre at the Singapore Zoological Gardens.* ③

Top, left and below: *The 28ha (69-acre) Singapore Zoological Gardens is home to many animal species, including tigers, the North American racoon and these baby chimps.*

Right: *Singapore's Changi Airport* ⑲ *has a reputation of being one of the finest airports in the world.* Biz Traveller *magazine (New Zealand), for example, voted Changi Airport the best in the world, while the German and Asian-Pacific editions of* Business Traveller *voted it 'the world's favourite airport'.*

Right: *Situated 15 minutes from the ultramodern Changi Airport, Changi Village* ⑳ *has a surprisingly rustic setting. Here you can quaff an ice-cold beer or enjoy a satisfying cup of coffee in one of the open-air cafés.*

Left: *From the ferry point at Changi, you can take a boat to any one of the northern islands, including idyllic Ubin with its wonderful seafood restaurants.*

Opposite: *The Control Tower at Changi Airport is a familiar and widely publicized landmark in Singapore.*

Left: *Golf used to be a rich man's game. Today, it is played by many successful young executives on the island, despite the fact that it still costs a small fortune.*

This edition published in 2003
First published in 1996 by
New Holland (Publishers) Ltd
London • Cape Town • Sydney • Auckland

86 Edgware Road
London W2 2EA
United Kingdom

14 Aquatic Drive
Frenchs Forest, NSW 2086
Australia

80 McKenzie Street
Cape Town 8001
South Africa

218 Lake Road
Northcote, Auckland
New Zealand

Copyright © 1996, 2003 New Holland (Publishers) Ltd
Copyright © 1996, 2003 in text: Chew Yen Fook
Copyright © 1996, 2003 in photographs: individual photographers and/or their agents as follows.

PHOTOGRAPHIC CREDITS

New Holland Image Library (Shaen Adey), except for the following: **Agence France-Presse (Pictor)** p. 18; **Agence France-Presse (Roslan Rahman)** pp. 24–25; **Black Star (Patrick Lim)** pp. 19 (bottom), 54 (centre), 80; **Black Star (Ian Lloyd)** pp. 28 (centre), 43, 52 (bottom); **Black Star (Charles Moore)** p. 10 (bottom); **Black Star (Paul van Riel)** p. 19 (top); **David Bowden** pp 20 (above and above right), 30 (above left), 45 (top), 64 (left), 76 (bottom left), 51, 52 (left), 53, 55, 59 (above), 64 (below), 65, 66 (centre), 76 (bottom left); **Chew Yen Fook** pp. 4 (top and bottom right), 5 (centre right and bottom right), 65; **Jill Gocher** pp. 7 (top), 11 (top), 12 (top), 13 (bottom), 16 (bottom), 30 (above right), 31, 33, 45 (above and bottom), 46 (left centre and below), 50 (below and bottom), 52 (left), 53, 55, 59 (above), 64 (below), 65, 66 (centre), 78 (centre and bottom); **Patrick Lim** pp. 3 (bottom right), 6 (bottom left), 8 (top), 9 (top and centre right), 10 (centre and top), 11 (bottom), 14 (top), 15, 16 (top), 17, 19 (centre), 22 (top and centre), 48–49, 54 (top), 54 (bottom), 64 (above and bottom); **Struik Image Library (Andrew Bannister)** pp. 1, 2 (top right), 4 (bottom left), 7 (bottom), 16 (centre), 22 (bottom), 23, 37, 39 (bottom), 52 (second from bottom), 58, 62, 63 (top), 67, 68, 69 (top and centre), 74 (centre and bottom right), 75; **Travel Ink (Geoffrey Clive)** front cover.

All rights reserved. No part of this publication may be reproduced, stored in a retrieval system or transmitted, in any form or by any means, electronic, mechanical, photocopying, recording or otherwise, without the prior written permission of the publishers and copyright holders.

The Publishers would like to thank the Land Transport Authority for their help in updating the MRT/LRT information.

ISBN: 1 84330 477 5
2 4 6 8 10 9 7 5 3 1

Publishing manager: Mariëlle Renssen
Editor: Jane Maliepaard
Updates: Leizel Brown, Janine Cloete
Lauren Copley
Designer: Alix Gracie
Cartographer: John Loubser
Reproduction by: Hirt & Carter (Pty) Ltd
Printing and binding in Singapore: Tien Wah Press (Pte) Ltd